Where Darkness Turns to Light

Your laugh echoes like a silly tune,
While we dance around like we own the moon.
Tripping over pillows, landing on dreams,
The night is ours bursting at the seams.

Who needs a film? Our stories are gold,
Each twist and turn is hilariously bold.
I forgot the plot, but who really cares?
With you by my side, there's laughter that flares.

The Caress of Night's Realms

Whispers of cheese float through the air,
As we share tales of socks that don't pair.
The stars giggle at our sleepy eyes,
As we scheme to catch the pizza pie.

Your hand tickles as we softly chat,
Dueling with pillows, just like cats.
The clock says late, but we don't mind,
In this cozy chaos, true joy we find.

Lost in the Tranquility of You

Such funny dreams drift at the edge,
Where wishes bounce like a trampoline ledge.
I trip on thoughts, you burst out in glee,
In this secret world, just you and me.

A dance-off erupts for zero applause,
As we twirl between laughs and silly flaws.
The moon peeks in, it's quite the sight,
Even the stars giggle at our delight.

The Heartbeat of Our Togetherness

In your embrace, I wiggle and squirm,
Two tangled bodies, a cozy term.
More like a pretzel, less like a hug,
Nestled together, like a bug in a rug.

Your snore is the soundtrack, quite the delight,
It echoes like thunder, oh what a night!
I poke you awake, just to complain,
Yet here we still are, doing the same.

Dusk's Lullaby

Outside the moon winks and plays peek-a-boo,
Yet it's your sleepy face that's my favorite view.
As you snore like a lion, I try hard to hold,
Laughter erupting, this story's retold.

Pajamas all twisted, socks on the floor,
We argue who's hogging the blankets for sure.
Temperature rising, our dance is a whirl,
You're my best giggle, my one and only girl.

The Art of Holding Silence

Silence wraps 'round, like a cozy old quilt,
But then you let out, a small squeaky guilt.
Your expression is priceless, pure comedic gold,
In our quiet moment, hilarity unfold.

We both try to whisper, yet laugh so much loud,
Sharing our secrets, like kids in a crowd.
Your face when I tickle, it's truly a sight,
In our silly stillness, we dance through the night.

Dreams Woven with the Moon's Thread

As dreams weave their magic, we travel through jest,
To a land where your laughter is always the best.
You ride on the unicorn, I play the flute,
A fairy tale ending, with you in a suit.

Awake from our visions, it's a chuckle parade,
Your hair's a wild mess, mischief displayed.
In the hall of the night, where giggles don't cease,
We reign as the monarchs, of laugh-filled peace.

Elysium Found in Moonlit Hues

Under the stars, we try to dance,
Tripping on shoes, losing romance.
You laugh so hard, I lose my breath,
In moonlit hues, we flirt with death.

Your hair's a mess, but so am I,
Whispers of laughter, like sparks they fly.
Between the giggles, we plot and scheme,
In this chaotic, silly dream.

The Soft Glow of Shared Breath

Your snore's a tune, a quirky song,
I try to count sheep, but I'm wrong.
Each breath we share is filled with cheer,
And marshmallow dreams that disappear.

With popcorn crumbs strewn all around,
We roll and tumble, our hearts unbound.
In the glow of snacks, we find our way,
Together in giggles that sway and play.

Heartbeats Echoing in the Dark

A thumping race from dusk till dawn,
Trying to snuggle, but the blanket's gone.
Cuddled up close, it's a cozy plight,
Your foot's on my face, oh what a sight!

In whispers soft, we share our dreams,
While plotting snacks and silly schemes.
Every heartbeat's a comedy show,
In this dark room, our laughter grows.

Navigating the Abyss of Us

In this great abyss of pillows and pillows,
We chart our course with tickles and thrills.
Maps of laughter drawn with doodles fine,
As we sail through chaos, your hand in mine.

The abyss is deep, but so is the fun,
A nightly adventure never to shun.
Lost in our quirks, we swim like fish,
Navigating joy, one silly wish.

Where the World Fades Away

In a whirl of winks, we sway,
Chasing shadows, come what may.
Tickle fights with giggles galore,
Who needs sleep? We explore.

Jumps in pajamas, a cartwheel or two,
Living wild like a hamster in a brew.
Dreams spill out like a pizza slice,
Midnight snacks, oh, that sounds nice!

Pet goldfish join the crazy dance,
Winking at us, a fishy glance.
The moon chuckles as we trip and fall,
Lost in laughter, hear the night call.

With each silly face, we turn back time,
Jesters in the dark, oh what a rhyme!
Giggling low, we paint the sky,
Who needs blankets? We fly high!

Through the Veil of Dusk

As stars peek out to play hide and seek,
We whisper secrets, our faces peek.
Twinkling lights above, twirling around,
In our kingdom, silliness is crowned.

Under the blanket fort, we laugh like fools,
Giggling echoes, breaking all the rules.
Silly hats and funky socks on parade,
Creating quests in a pillow brigade.

With candy canes and chocolate dreams,
We sail on clouds, bursting at the seams.
The sundown bids us a playful tease,
In the quiet chaos, we find our ease.

Every giggle feels like a jest,
In a goofy dance, we find our rest.
With silly songs strumming our hearts,
In this twilight, we play our parts.

The Magic of a Breath Away

Poof! A dragon made of candy floss,
In this dreamland, we take the gloss.
Glittering wishes scatter like seeds,
Wordplay blooms into unexpected deeds.

Unicorns prance on a tater-tot street,
Laughter spills over, an endless treat.
Pegasus pancakes whisk us away,
To the land where sprinkles run the day.

A dance-off with raccoons in a band,
Dancing like nobody had it planned.
We tumble together, what a sight,
In this whimsical world, we ignite.

With giggles and charms, we weave the night,
Every silly moment feels just right.
A bubble of joy, we take a ride,
In magical moments, we confide.

Silhouettes Wrapped in Desire

In shadow plays, we twist and twirl,
With silly grins, let chaos swirl.
A marathon of chases 'round the room,
Dancing to laughter, lifting the gloom.

Our silhouettes against the light,
Like playful kittens, ready to bite.
Tangles of limbs, a curious dance,
In every fumble, we take a chance.

The clock strikes twelve; we craft a spell,
Making wishes, oh can you tell?
With bubblegum laughter filling the air,
Every glance shared, beyond compare.

Wrapped in moments, soft laughter hears,
Shadows whispering, shedding our fears.
In the glimmers of play, we find delight,
Captured forever in this playful night.

Hours Spun from Celestial Threads

When the clock strikes twelve, we frolic and play,
Tangled in laughter, we dance till the gray.
Stars are our witnesses, they giggle and twirl,
Time flies on wings, like a squeaky toy whirl.

Your silly sock puppet, it steals the show,
Winks at the fridge, where leftovers grow.
Every tick of the clock, a jest does emerge,
In the still of the night, our chuckles converge.

Entwined Beneath a Canopy of Stars

With marshmallow dreams and an ice cream dream,
We challenge each other to a pillow fight scheme.
Giggles erupt as we tumble and roll,
Under the moon's gaze, we lose our control.

You try to be serious, it's quite the charade,
But your snorts start a ruckus, plans start to fade.
In this cosmic cocoon, all worries feel small,
As we laugh at the universe, we conquer it all.

The Language of Stillness

In the quiet we whisper, with grins on our face,
Even the walls chuckle, it's quite the embrace.
Your gentle snoring is a melody sweet,
While I sneak in some snacks for a mid-night treat.

As the shadows dance lightly, we share little jests,
Like two silly geese, we forget all our quests.
In the hush of our fortress, the absurdity flows,
Life's a wacky sitcom, and we steal the shows.

Cradled by the Weight of Night

The blankets are tangled, we're mummies for sure,
Both craving a snack, but too comfy to move.
With a crunch and a munch, the giggling ensues,
Our sleepy adventure, a candy buffet's muse.

Caught in this sappy, delightful delight,
You've got crumbs on your nose, and it's quite the sight.
With whispers and chuckles, the world fades away,
In the softest of chaos, we're here to stay!

Fluid Moments of Quietude

In the dim light, we share a snack,
Crumbs like stars, scattered on the track.
Laughter bubbles, silly as can be,
Your cheesy grin is the best sight to see.

Pizza rolls dance in the microwave's hum,
My dreams of gourmet, but this is way fun.
We countdown the seconds, like kids on a quest,
Who knew midnight munchies could feel like a fest?

Time takes a twist, moments start to bend,
Every silly joke seems to be the trend.
With you by my side, I could dive a bit deep,
In the warmth of your laughter, it's hard not to leap.

So here's to the quirks and the giggles we share,
Beneath the neon lights, we float through the air.
In these charming hours, with our own little play,
Let the night linger longer, that's all I can say!

Serene Echoes of Your Presence

Your snoring is symphonic, a lullaby loud,
A serenade ringing, oh how I feel proud.
Dreaming of sugar plums or maybe a pie,
But waking to roars, I can't help but sigh.

In this cozy chaos, pillows are our throne,
A fortress of laughter, we've truly outgrown.
Witty remarks fly like birds in the sky,
Who needs the moonlight when you're my guy?

Together we twiddle our thumbs in the haze,
Time seems to giggle, it's stuck in a daze.
Jokes tumble like raindrops, soft on the floor,
Every smirk implores me to love you even more.

With the world outside quiet, we giggle away,
In our own little bubble, where we choose to play.
As the clock softly whispers, "just stay for tonight,"
In these serene echoes, everything feels right!

Beneath a Canopy of Dreams

Under the covers, we conjure a show,
Pillow fights erupt, like banners they flow.
Your wit is a weapon, though I'm armed with glee,
In this grand battle, I'm the mightiest bee!

Spinning wild tales of dragons and knights,
With popcorn galore, we conquer the nights.
You're the king of nonsense, I'm the queen of fun,
Together we rule, till the dawn makes us run.

Chasing our shadows, we dance in the dark,
The giggles erupt like the first little spark.
Wrapped in a whirlwind of dreams rich and bold,
Every shared moment feels like pure gold.

So let's weave our laughter in the fabric of time,
Crafting sweet stories within every chime.
In this playful land, every slumber is bliss,
For who needs the world when we have this kiss?

Where Time Stands Still

Tick tock, it stops, as we share a glance,
Ice cream, our partner in this silly dance.
With sprinkles of laughter, we giggle and spin,
What magic awaits, with your goofy grin?

The clock melts away as we climb into dreams,
Floating through mazes, life bursting at seams.
With quirky adventures that know no end,
Every minute with you feels like time to spend.

So here we are, in this comical fight,
Where the night wears a mask, full of delight.
With wit for the ages, our smiles unite,
In the shadow of moonbeams, all feels just right.

Each moment a treasure, each sigh a new song,
In this world of whimsy, together we belong.
So let's dive through the twilight, with hearts that are bold,
In this playful realm, we'll never grow old!

The Palette of Twilight Dreams

In shades of blue, we laugh and play,
As starlit jokes sway night away.
With paintbrush lips, we slip and slide,
In canvassed warmth, our hearts collide.

With glittered wishes, we draw a line,
Between the silly and the divine.
Your laugh's the color that lights my way,
In hues of twilight, we'll always stay.

Frequencies of Love in the Dark

Our giggles echo, a radio tune,
Through midnight's whispers, under the moon.
With funny signals and silly beats,
We dance in silence, but joy repeats.

Your quirky smiles are my favorite sound,
In this dark groove, true love is found.
We hum our hits, the chart-topper's dream,
In laughter's rhythm, we're a perfect team.

The Slow Dance of Our Spirits

In two left feet, we sway and glide,
With every stumble, our hearts collide.
A waltz of whimsy in this embrace,
With ticklish turns, we set the pace.

Your silly spin makes me want to laugh,
In the slow dance, you're my better half.
With arms like ribbons, we twist and twirl,
What a delight in our joyous whirl!

Nights Carved in Velvet

In velvet whispers, we make our art,
Scribbling laughter straight from the heart.
Under the fabric of midnight skies,
We stitch together the silliest lies.

With a jump and bump, we craft our tale,
In this strange world, we'll never fail.
Your quirky ideas make starlight bloom,
In soft, warm shadows, we banish gloom.

The Language of Unrushed Moments

Your snore in the night sounds like a song,
A symphony played all night long.
I trip over socks, laugh at the scene,
Life's a comedy when you're my routine.

Whispers of dreams as we both snooze,
You steal the sheets, what have I to lose?
Cuddles turn into wrestling matches of fun,
Under the moon, we're the only ones.

With popcorn in hand, we share a movie,
You dance in your sleep, but oh so groovy.
I plot my escape to the edge of the bed,
But your arm pulls me back, the scene's never dead.

In pajamas so bright, we lounge until noon,
The cat's in a heap, joined in our tune.
With laughter and memes, we drift into space,
Two clowns in love in our jammies embrace.

Stealing Glances at Forever

Your socks don't match, but who even cares?
In a world built on laughter, we'll go anywhere.
We trade sleepy smiles, a quirky ballet,
As morning light filters, chasing the gray.

The coffee's a mess, the mug's looking grim,
But here in our chaos, the joy's never slim.
With cereal rainbows splashed on each plate,
We feast on absurdity, savoring fate.

You steal a glance, my heart does a flip,
Your face is a canvas, funny in quips.
With inside jokes that only we know,
Step by goofy step, we let our love grow.

We juggle our dreams like clowns in a ring,
With giggles as background music we sing.
Through playful exchanges, we find our way,
Together in laughter and love every day.

Navigating Through Infinite Calm

Our blanket fort's up, we're kings of the night,
In pillow fortresses, we're ready for flight.
With snacks piled high and movies to binge,
Adventures await with a whimsical fringe.

You give me that look when the plot starts to flatten,
But each scene's a riddle, and laughter's our weapon.
With popcorn as ammo, we battle the dull,
In this fortress of laughter, we give it our all.

We race to the fridge for midnight delight,
But trip on a cat—oh, what a sight!
In this dance of chaos, we twirl and we slip,
The universe giggles at our silly trip.

Under the starlight, we plot our next scheme,
In a world made of dreams, we're the ultimate team.
With laughter and snacks, our spirits take flight,
Navigating calm, love's a joyous delight.

Beyond the Twilight's Reach

As dusk wraps us in a whimsical embrace,
We find our rhythm in this cozy space.
Each tick of the clock, a comedic play,
In this twilight theatre, we always stay.

Your jokes are my sunshine, warming the air,
As shadows pirouette without a single care.
With hiccuping laughter, we chase back the dark,
Turning endless silence into our own spark.

In mismatched pajamas, we plot our escape,
Sneaking snacks from the kitchen, a grand little cape.
With giggles and grace, we quietly scheme,
This is our kingdom, where nothing's a dream.

As stars shine above, we count each one bold,
While concocting tales that never grow old.
With tickles and whispers shared in the night,
Beyond twilight's reach, everything feels right.

Kindred Spirits in the Night Air

Beneath the stars, we laugh and roam,
Searching for snacks, far from home.
You steal the fries from my far hand,
Pretending it's all part of your plan.

We dance like fools, no rhythm found,
Tripping over shoes left on the ground.
You claim to be the king of style,
Yet keep losing battles, all the while.

The moon shines bright, a spotlight rare,
As we juggle donuts in the air.
You drop one quick, it lands with a splat,
Now there's icing on your favorite hat.

Let's keep the giggles, let worries slide,
In this wacky ride, I'll be your guide.
With every chuckle, the world feels right,
You and I, the jesters of the night.

Wrapped in the Essence of Twilight

In twilight's glow, we share a bite,
An ice cream cone, a silly fight.
You say it's yours, but here we go,
With half a scoop on your nose, oh no!

The crickets chirp their silly tunes,
While we debate which planet's a goon.
You shout, "Uranus!" with no delay,
And I burst out laughing, what can I say?

The stars align as we sip our sodas,
You snicker at life, and I join the bliss.
With a splash here and a fizz over there,
We paint the night, choosing joy over care.

As daylight fades, let's dance 'til dawn,
With goofy moves, our worries are gone.
Wrapped in giggles, we twirl and sway,
These sweet moments, we'll never betray.

Surrenders Beneath the Moon's Gaze

Under the moon, we play our game,
Whispering secrets that no one can tame.
You take my pen, and doodle away,
Drawing mustaches on my face with no delay.

A midnight feast of cereal and cake,
You claim it's gourmet, for goodness' sake!
We toast with milk, and laugh 'til we snort,
With our kitchen chaos, it's a wild sport.

The night unfolds, with silly debates,
About the best kind of snack on plates.
You argue chips while I swear by cheese,
But all we can do is laugh with ease.

As the moon winks in prideful glee,
We surrender to joy, just you and me.
Let's dance in the kitchen, just us and the light,
Chasing dreams through this whimsical night.

The Spaces Between Heartbeats

In the cozy gaps where laughter sleeps,
We share our silly secrets, the joy that leaps.
You make a face, a silly little grin,
The world feels lighter, with you it's a win.

The silence screams with quirky charms,
As we pretend we're superheroes with arms.
You drag a cape and stumble around,
While I can't help but laugh at the sound.

In those quiet spaces, your giggles break,
Like hidden treasures that laughter makes.
We pop like bubbles, a bubbly surprise,
In the glow of the night, your mischief flies.

So let's keep moving through giggles and sighs,
In the rhythm of hearts where pure joy lies.
The spaces between, our laughter's embrace,
A memory wrapped in this delightful place.

The Heart's Voyage Under Starlight

In a boat made of dreams, we float,
Rowing with the rhythm of a goat.
Stars twinkle like our silly jokes,
Dancing as we dodge the yokes.

The moon is our lamp, quite aloof,
Casting shadows on our goof.
With giggles slipping from our lips,
We navigate with comic quips.

Waves whisper secrets of our fun,
As we pretend to weigh a ton.
But worry not, it's just a game,
In this laughable love, we feel the same.

So let's sail 'til the break of light,
With silly banter, our hearts take flight.
For each wave brings a splash of cheer,
In this voyage, forever near.

Surrounded by Echoes of You

In a room of echoes, your laugh lingers,
Tickling us both with mischievous fingers.
Every corner hums with playful tease,
Ballooning laughter carried by the breeze.

You trip on words, I trip on air,
Both of us tangled in lack of care.
Our playful banter, a glorious tune,
Laughing at shadows that dance with the moon.

The walls giggle softly, don't keep it quiet,
As we spin stories, a delightful riot.
Pillow fights bring giggly skirmishes,
And every corner holds our sweet wishes.

So let's paint this room with splashes of glee,
Lives intertwined, just you and me.
Under the smiles and soft-hearted view,
We craft our echoes, forever true.

Embracing the Quietude of Dusk

When the sun dips low, we act like fools,
Crafting shadows, forgetting the rules.
In this twilight zone, our giggles collide,
As we fumble through moments, side by side.

The crickets play tunes, we dance on the floor,
With snacks in hand, we tumble once more.
Who knew a sunset could spark such delight,
As we trip on the grass, deep into the night.

The stars peek out, but we've made our mess,
With each stumble, our laughter grows less.
We hug like two blobs in a sticky embrace,
In the quietude, we find our place.

So let's bask in the dusk, mischief our guide,
With silly smiles and love undenied.
Under the canopy of a fading hue,
Ever closer, it's just me and you.

A Reverie of Midnight Shadows

In shadows deep where whispers play,
We giggle softly, night turns to day.
With pillow forts made of dreams and threads,
Our laughter echoes while the world heads to beds.

We play hide and seek with the fading light,
Creaky floors groan as we plot our flight.
In our midnight realm, a surreal parade,
Each silly stunt in this escapade.

While coffee brews in the kitchen nearby,
We make wishes on sparks that fly high.
Bouncing ideas like balls in the air,
As shadows dance, carefree without a care.

So let's toast to the joy this night brings,
With silly shenanigans and makeshift wings.
In a realm where laughter throws its net,
Forever youth in a moonlit duet.

Whispers of Twilight's Embrace

In the twilight, we do sway,
With snacks and games till break of day.
Your laughter spills like fizzy drink,
Together we puzzle, then overthink.

Tickles and giggles fill the space,
As we jump and dance in a silly chase.
You steal my fries, then give a grin,
Oh, what joy, this playful sin!

A pillow fort we build in haste,
Where superhero capes we taste.
With silly stories spun so bright,
The world fades into pure delight.

We'll forge our myths, so slightly grand,
With all the quirks we've carefully planned.
In this little bubble, we find our ease,
Letting loose, oh, how it please!

Shadows Wrapped in Your Warmth

In your warm hug I find my thrill,
Dragging pillows up the hill.
With popcorn fights and silly faces,
We make the dark the best of places.

Socks on the floor, a wild array,
Falling over as we sway.
The shadows dance, we spin like tops,
In this whirl of joy, the laughter never stops.

We're like two clowns in a circus tent,
Trading jokes and the time we spent.
With a wink and a nudge, we laugh so loud,
Creating a shimmer that breaks the cloud.

As we whisper secrets, thoughts take flight,
In the glow of the moon, we ignite the night.
A comedic duo wrapped tight like toast,
In this midnight warmth, we toast to the most!

Starlit Serenades of Togetherness

Beneath the stars, we sing our tune,
With off-key melodies, we chase the moon.
Each twinkling note makes room for cheer,
As we belt our dreams, nothing to fear.

Silly hats and goofy glasses,
We strut about as the time passes.
With every chorus, giggles clash,
In this cozy nook, our hearts just smash.

You dance like no one's watching us,
With every stumble, it's hard to trust.
Yet in this frolic, we find our bliss,
Planting a funny, stolen kiss.

From this canvas bright, our laughter grows,
In moments shared, each story flows.
In goofy antics, side by side,
We craft a night that will never hide!

A Canvas of Midnight Emotions

Canvas laid, we paint the night,
With splashes of joy, oh what a sight!
Your brush stirs chaos, colors collide,
As we masterpiece our silly ride.

Dripping laughter on the floor,
You challenge me just to say 'more.'
With every swipe, we wear a grin,
In this madness, we always win.

A sip of cocoa, a giggly toast,
You in your pajamas, raising a ghost.
Between the strokes, we plot our schemes,
Filling the hours with ridiculous dreams.

So let's throw the paint, a vibrant spree,
In these midnight hours, just you and me.
This canvas speaks of joy and fun,
Our masterpiece shines, forever won!

Chasing Dreams Underneath the Stars

Under a blanket, we lie with glee,
Counting the stars, just you and me.
Your snoring loudly, a symphony deep,
While I'm wide awake, trying not to weep.

The constellations giggle, twinkling bright,
As we debate if it's really night.
Pizza delivery lost on the way,
It's an adventure, come what may!

With weeds like gardens, our shoes in a mess,
My heart races on, must confess.
You toss and turn, like a fish out of sea,
Leaving me wondering, will you wake up with me?

But even in chaos, I'm blissfully lost,
For a night like this, oh, what a cost!
A masterpiece painted, with laughter and smiles,
Let's chase those wild dreams for a few extra miles.

Midnight Secrets Held Tight

Whispers of secrets fill up the room,
While cats conspire, preparing to zoom.
You claim you love, "cereal at three,"
But I know your heart is set on that tea.

Tick-tock goes the clock, a silent ninja,
As we dance in pajamas, like wild flamingos.
Your tickle attacks are truly a threat,
Leave it to me to laugh and forget!

Fingers interlaced, we plot our next heist,
Should we steal cookies? Oh, that sounds nice.
But crumbs on the bed, oh what a mess,
Blame it on me, I must confess!

In the chaos, we find your missing sock,
Wrapped together, we fear the clock.
Don't let the morning bring this fun to a close,
For who needs sleep when we've got this prose?

Love's Infinite Twilight

In the quiet hours, your laugh fills the air,
As I steal your fries without a care.
Your jokes are goofy, but they make me smile,
Let's stretch this twilight just a little while.

Dancing in shadows, we twirl and we sway,
Your two left feet lead my heart astray.
The moon rolls its eyes, as it watches us play,
Whispering soft dreams, that won't fade away.

But just as romance begins to take flight,
You trip on the rug, oh what a sight!
With a puff of laughter, we tumble and fall,
Covered in giggles, we'll conquer it all.

Your hair's a wild mess, and mine's in a bun,
These moments together, we're having such fun.
So let's hold this twilight, let's never let go,
For in love's crazy dance, we're the stars of the show!

The Infinite Loop of Us

Round and round we spin in this loop,
You munch on popcorn, while I sip on soup.
Your weird little dances make my heart race,
I wouldn't trade this for the whole human race.

Binge-watching shows, in mismatched attire,
You laugh at my jokes, though they might retire.
With each silly moment, our bond starts to grow,
Like unicycle cats juggling in a show!

When shadows creep in and the lights start to dim,
We steal midnight snacks, on a whimsical whim.
Crumbs on the sofa, a treasure we've found,
In the deep of the night, our laughter's the sound.

So here's to this loop, so funny and bright,
In the tale of our hearts, we savor the night.
With our quirks and our dreams in a lovely embrace,
We're forever entwined, lost in our space.

A Tapestry of Unspoken Words

In the dark, we share our snacks,
Whispers dance along with laughs.
You steal my fries, I steal your drink,
In this cozy space, we just wink.

Your snore's a symphony, offbeat and loud,
As I try to dance, you sleep like a cloud.
Between the giggles and the playful chats,
We build skyscrapers from pizza and mats.

Where the Stars Write Our Story

Outside, the moon plays peekaboo,
While we make shadows, me and you.
Your stories sprout like mushrooms in rain,
While I roll my eyes, still entertained.

Counting sheep, like counting debts,
But you'd rather debate on unicorn pets.
In this whimsical world, we create such joy,
With playful banter, never coy.

In the Womb of Night's Embrace

Warm blankets wrap us like a hug,
While you claim the pillow, give me a tug.
Your dreams are wild, a circus, I bet,
Mine's just me, trying to catch my pet.

You show me tricks with your hair, I laugh,
Turning my side into your personal half.
Our silly dances and awkward sways,
Make this night feel like a game we play.

Veiled Secrets of Affection

In the stillness, a grin fights the dark,
You mumble secrets, like a playful lark.
With every giggle, our souls intertwine,
Warding off boredom, so divine.

Now shall we solve this jigsaw of fate?
Or just build a fort and procrastinate?
With snacks as our treasure, we plot our schemes,
In this cocoon of laughter, we weave our dreams.

The Infinite Tapestry of Souls

In cozy depths of couch potato land,
We share the blanket like it's all we planned.
Your snacks are sacred, but mine take flight,
Between the giggles, we strategize the bite.

I lost my footing, tripped on your shoe,
You laughed so hard, I almost flew.
With every stumble, laughter reigns,
Two clumsy souls, no sense of gains.

Our laughter echoes, a cosmic mess,
You claim I'm charming, but who's to guess?
In this quirky dance of left and right,
We twirl through chaos, a silly sight.

So here we are, lost in our jest,
With mismatched socks and a playful quest.
In this tapestry of goofy delight,
We weave our souls, into the night.

Unraveled in a Twilight Embrace

Under the stars, mischief takes flight,
Your pillow fortress is quite the sight.
We plot on snacks, the heist of the day,
In shadows we bunker, come what may.

I dubbed you king of the couch throne wide,
But secret snacks were my crafty pride.
You wave your hand like a seasoned pro,
While crumbs betray me in the afterglow.

The clock ticks on, but it knows no bounds,
In our bubble, lost time surrounds.
With every punchline, we giggle and sway,
Tonight's mischief turns dull into bright play.

So let's draw giggles 'til dawn takes flight,
In this haven where laughter ignites.
We'll revel in chaos, let time stand still,
In this twilight embrace, we'll laugh at will.

Silhouettes Dancing in the Night

We're shadows wavering in the pale moonlight,
Your dance moves equal a clumsy fright.
A twirl, a stumble, you steal my breath,
In this comedy, we laugh at death.

With every leap, a new joke unfolds,
Your hip-hop flair? Oh, it's pure gold!
We bust a move in this wobbly spree,
Our silhouettes sway, wild and carefree.

I snort at the sight, hope you don't mind,
Your rhythm should be labeled 'one of a kind.'
We break the silence with playful shouts,
In this quirky ballet, it's no doubt.

So let's dance on, 'neath sky's watchful gaze,
With laughter and rhyme, we set ablaze.
For in each misstep, joy shall ignite,
We'll twirl as silhouettes, lost in delight.

Captured Moments of Starlit Whispers

You whisper secrets of chocolate delight,
Swiping my treats in the dead of the night.
We giggle and plot in this starlit chat,
While visions of snacks blend with silly spat.

You say, "Just one!" as crumbs hit the floor,
But the cookie jar calls, it can't be ignored.
With every sly smile, we wander the line,
'Twixt friends and thieves, oh, what a design!

In this dance of snacks under the sky,
We toast to spirit, let laughter fly.
As moonlight glimmers on our cheerful raid,
Moments etched forever, in laughter's parade.

So gather your giggles, let mischief arise,
Our starlit whispers, the best of all ties.
In this pocket of joy where mischief abounds,
Captured in laughter, our friendship resounds.

Mornings Born from Midnight Bliss

As the clock strikes two, we snack on cake,
Sipping our drinks, for goodness' sake!
You tell me jokes that don't quite land,
I laugh so hard, spill mint in hand.

Pillow fights in the dim moon's glow,
Your pajama pants are too tight, whoa!
We dance like fools to a song off-key,
Can we survive tomorrow? Let's wait and see.

When dawn approaches, we hide and squeal,
Under the covers, we make a deal.
To steal some moments, carefree and wild,
Pretending we're still that mischievous child.

But as I yawn, your snore's a charm,
A silly symphony, my midnight balm.
Morning's light peeks, we're still in a haze,
As we tangle in sheets, lost in this daze.

A Symphony of Night's Caress

The stars above twinkle with glee,
Your dance moves make me beam like a bee.
Socks not matching, you spin around,
Like a butterfly lost, yet joyfully found.

A blanket fort built with snacks in hand,
You munch on chips while we bravely band.
Your laugh, contagious, a giggly sound,
Echoes in darkness, pure bliss all around.

With shadows creeping, we hide from sight,
Pretending we're ninjas, oh, what a fright!
You trip over pillows, we roll on the floor,
Who knew that laughter could open such doors?

But morning's approach is a thief in the night,
As we giggle through yawns, holding on tight.
We'll snooze till the sun claims the day,
For our nighttime shenanigans keep blues at bay.

Whispers of Midnight Embrace

Whispers and giggles fill up the air,
As we plot our adventure without a care.
Wearing your shirt that's three sizes too big,
You try to dance, but boy, you're a twig!

The clock ticks slowly, or is it just me?
Your sleepy eyelids, a sight to see.
We tell ghost stories that make no sense,
Scaring ourselves with every pretense.

Now wrapped in blankets, cozy and tight,
You yawn and sparkle, oh what a sight!
Midnight mischief, with every embrace,
Turns into laughter—a warm, gentle race.

But soon we'll crash, with dreams intertwined,
Counting adventures that we've designed.
So let's tuck in, with a smile so wide,
For tomorrow will bring a new silly ride.

Shadows of Twilight Caress

Caught in twilight, we laugh to the tune,
Of crickets serenading beneath the moon.
You drop the popcorn all over the floor,
While I tease you and beg for just more!

With your goofy face and my wobbly dance,
We take on the night, oh what a chance!
Tickle fights burst into giggles so sweet,
We break out the snacks, now isn't this neat?

Your snorts and chuckles blend into the air,
A humor so rich, it's beyond compare.
We chat about aliens and worlds so grand,
Dreaming of journeys across time's great land.

But mornings are sneaking, we hear their call,
As shadows retreat and we feel the sprawls.
Yet these twilight hours, we'll forever recall,
Every weird moment, every silly sprawl.

The Timelessness of a Breath

In the dark, our laughter rings,
Like cats dressed up as kings.
We fumble, trip, and hit the floor,
While searching for snacks and nothing more.

You steal my fries, I pout, I grin,
In this silly dance, we both begin.
With pillows piled up to the sky,
We trade our dreams for a late-night pie.

The clock ticks louder, it's nearly three,
Yet here we are, just you and me.
Your snoring sounds like a beastly roar,
I wonder why I still want more.

As dawn breaks in, a sleepy sum,
We never said this night was done.
With yawns and sighs, and chuckles so bright,
We laugh off the madness of our night flight.

Sailing Through Still Waters

We sail on dreams, not a single wave,
With snacks in hand, we think we're brave.
A rubber duck floats by, oh dear,
Who knew that bath time could bring such cheer?

The oars are missing, but who needs those?
We paddle with laughter, it's how it goes.
With splashes galore, we make quite the mess,
Yet hearts feel light, and we couldn't care less.

A seal pops up, looking quite absurd,
It claps its fins, and it seems to concur.
We toast with sippy cups, best kind of brew,
Adventuring gladly, just me and you.

The moon laughs at us, we wave back bold,
In this goofy galley, our tale unfolds.
As time flows sweet, we find delight,
Sailing through giggles, the stars shining bright.

A Dance Beneath Celestial Canopies

Beneath the stars, we trip and sway,
Two clumsy fools, in our own ballet.
I stepped on your foot, you flung your drink,
Under the cosmos, we can't help but blink.

With moves like jelly, we twist and spin,
Trying to hide just how much we grin.
The fireflies join, they twinkle and flash,
As we twirl and spin, hearts ready to clash.

Your hat flies off, a sight so grand,
I chase it down—it's part of the plan!
Racing through shadows, laughing with glee,
A dance with the night, just you and me.

With giggles bursting, the moon winks down,
Two goofballs under a blanket crown.
As music plays softly from the trees,
We dance and we dream, we do as we please.

The Unraveling of Collapsed Time

Time turns to jelly, what a funny state,
You grin at me, and I can't hesitate.
We giggle at clocks that seem to stall,
As minutes twist and sometimes fall.

With midnight snacks, we craft our lore,
Cookies, cake, and maybe more.
The fridge beams proudly, its light our guide,
In this wacky world, we can't hide.

Jumping through hours like they're made of cheese,
We're waltzing with shadows, with utmost ease.
Each tick's a giggle, each tock's a dance,
In this chaotic game, we take our chance.

As dawn paints skies with sleepy pinks,
We laugh at the night's strange little kinks.
In the unraveling, joy is sublime,
With you by my side, there's no such thing as time.

A Symphony Beneath the Stars

Under the moon, my socks take flight,
Squirrels dance, they're quite a sight.
Your laughter echoes through the night,
With each bump, it's pure delight.

The crickets join our merry band,
And try to keep up on demand.
We trip on dreams, a clumsy boat,
While stars above begin to gloat.

With every giggle, the world spins round,
You drop your ice cream on the ground.
I promise, it's not just the wine,
You're the punchline and that's just fine!

As fireflies wink, we can't ignore,
The snacks we brought now hit the floor.
So grab that pie, don't let it roll,
Living like this is our ultimate goal!

Echoes of a Starlit Serenade

A serenade in a funky key,
Your feet dance, oh the jubilee!
Neon lights flash, we sing too loud,
Our voices blend, it's quite the crowd.

A ukulele on your knee,
You strum a tune, oh so free.
The neighbors yell, 'truce for the night!',
We chuckle while they turn off the light.

With popcorn flying, we make a mess,
Who knew that laughter could feel like chess?
You serve a laugh, I can't attend,
Trip over shadows, our giggles blend.

The sky's our stage, we'll forever play,
Cheesy lines at the end of the day.
So let's spin under this cosmic dome,
In this comedy, we've truly found home!

Wrapped in the Silk of Dreams

Tangled sheets, a pillow fight,
You thwacked my head with all your might.
Feathers fly, we laugh and roll,
In this chaos, we find our soul.

With silly faces and goofy grins,
You challenge me; oh, where to begin?
The nighttime world veils in a haze,
We lose ourselves in this playful maze.

I'll steal your snacks, you'll steal my dreams,
Your bewildered stare, or so it seems.
While giggling shadows play peek-a-boo,
Every moment feels so refreshingly new.

As dawn begins to break our spree,
You yawn and stretch, but still, let's agree.
These silly nights make our hearts beam,
Wrapped together in this joyful dream!

When Moonlight Dances With You

Moonlight spins in your curly hair,
We twirl like dancers, without a care.
But wait! You step on my big toe,
With a grin like that, I dare not show!

Beneath the stars, we build a fort,
With snacks and laughs, who needs support?
The ruling laws? Just giggles and sighs,
As gummy bears moonwalk on the pies!

Our shadow puppets craft their tales,
Silly antics that never fail.
You claim to be a wizard bright,
But even your spells can't stop the night!

Time slips by like a wobbly tune,
With hiccups and chuckles beneath the moon.
So let's raise our cups to whimsical flights,
In this grand play of our starry nights!

Reflections of Us in the Moonlight

We danced to jokes in the silver glow,
With shadows laughing as they stole the show.
Your laughter echoed like a silly tune,
While crickets chirped beneath the silly moon.

A pillow fight broke out on the spree,
As feathers floated, a comical sea.
We rolled and tumbled, all giggles and glee,
With dreams as wild as a dancing bee.

Our marshmallow plans melted into the night,
Dreaming of adventures with no care in sight.
The stars were spies, oh what a sight to view,
As you told me tales both silly and true.

In each muffled snort and snuggle so tight,
We found our rhythm, all wrongs felt so right.
These golden hours with you by my side,
Left echoes of laughter, our hearts open wide.

Holding You Beyond the Threshold

At the door, we lingered, caught in a snare,
A dance of clumsy feet, kisses in the air.
As we slipped on shoes, a tangled embrace,
Each moment a giggle, like we're lost in space.

You turned to me, and I burst out in glee,
Tripping on words, then on my own knee.
With popcorn dreams and wild plans to roam,
We held each other, our own little home.

The dog looked puzzled, a frown on his face,
Wondering when we would leave this place.
But we laughed instead, and the night rolled on,
Your smile like sunshine, into the dawn.

As we wandered far, we lost track of time,
Jokes flowing like rivers, in a rhythm and rhyme.
In this blissful chaos, let them all see,
Together, forever, it's just you and me.

A Universe of Soft Touches

In a galaxy spun of fuzzy delight,
We discovered plush planets in pillow flight.
You cheeked your way to another grand joke,
With laughter like stardust, our hearts nearly broke.

A comet of kisses shot past in a blink,
The coffee table turned into a pink sink.
We plunged through portals of giggles and sighs,
As mysteries danced beneath shimmering skies.

Swirling in visions of a world unconfined,
Where every soft touch left a sparkle behind.
Our feet tapped with rhythm, a cosmic charade,
In this universe built on the love we had made.

And as we floated, stardust in our hair,
Time giggled with us, banished each care.
The night air whispered, in chuckles and streams,
We built a cosmos of silly, sweet dreams.

A Trusting Heart Beneath Stars

Under a blanket of glimmering lore,
We sat in giggles, who could ask for more?
With popcorn in hand, we shared all our fears,
Then burst into laughter while wiping our tears.

Your stories spun around in whimsical loops,
As we watched tiny satellites dance in groups.
The earth beneath us, our legs all a tangle,
Connected by laughter, love's sweetest wrangle.

A breeze whispered secrets, oh where could they be?
We traded them back, you shared one with me.
In this quiet moment, under a starry quilt,
We built a fortress of joy, love, and guilt.

We chuckled at dreams that were wild and absurd,
A symphony of laughter, not one word unheard.
In the arms of the night, where silliness reigns,
Our trusting hearts danced, breaking all the chains.

Lullabies Beneath the Cosmos

Stars twinkle like we're on a spree,
Your snore is like a symphony.
Blankets tangled with much delight,
We giggle softly through the night.

Moonlight spills on our pillow fight,
Your hair's a mess, a funny sight.
Dreams mix up in silly ways,
As we chuckle through the haze.

We count the sheep, but lose track,
Then wrestle pillows, sparks set back.
The clock is stuck, but who will mind?
With you here, joy's what I find.

Cosmic giggles dance in the air,
With whispered dreams that go to share.
Each laugh, a note in soft refrain,
Here in the galaxy of our mundane.

When Time Stands Still with You

Tick-tock, the clock's gone lazy,
With you here, I feel so hazy.
Minutes stretch like tales we spin,
In this game, who needs to win?

You steal my fries, I take your ear,
Time melts, nothing's ever sheer.
Fingers sticky, laughter loud,
We pop the popcorn, feeling proud.

Every second turns to glee,
In a world that's just for we.
You make faces, I can't resist,
Oh, how can I not laugh at this?

The clock's a joke, a sidekick neat,
When you're around, the time's complete.
In goofy moments, we just sway,
Forever stuck in this ballet.

The Unbroken Thread of Dusk

Dusk wraps us in a silly hug,
With empty cups, we start to chug.
Each whispered joke, a thread we weave,
In this twilight, we believe.

Your sleepy smile, a winning game,
I trip and fall, but you just claim,
We dance like fools, all in good fun,
Under the moon, we're on the run.

The stretch of night is ours to claim,
With blooper reels, it's all the same.
You blink too slowly, I can't contain,
The laughter spills like sweet champagne.

With each mishap, a melody,
In this chaos, we find our spree.
Unbroken threads through night's delight,
Silly mistakes that feel just right.

Flickering Hearts in a Nocturnal Dance

In shadows cast, we twirl and sway,
Your clumsy steps lead us astray.
With flashing lights, a disco scene,
Our hearts beat wild, but it's routine.

You stumble and laugh, I trip and snort,
In this odd ball, we find our sport.
The night unfolds in wobbly moves,
Love's rhythm is what we approve.

We keep the beat with silly flair,
Each spinning twist, an answered prayer.
Under the stars, we spin the night,
In our mad dance, everything's right.

A flicker here, a giggle there,
With every misstep, we're well aware.
Hearts uplifted in playful trance,
Together forever, in our jolly dance.

The Allure of Infinite Hush

In the stillness we find our grace,
Whispers tickle like a warm embrace.
Your snoring's a lullaby, softly played,
As I plot revenge with a pillow cascade.

Moonlight dances on your sleepy face,
While I try to sneak away, but I'm out of place.
The blanket's a puzzle, we're tangled tight,
I check the clock; are we winning this fight?

Your feet are cold, they seek my heat,
A nightly battle with cozy retreat.
My dreams of freedom swiftly dissipate,
As I grin and bear this cuddle fate.

In this quiet chaos, we find delight,
Competing for space till the morning light.
A circus of hearts in a small-sized bed,
Who knew love could be so joyously led?

Unbroken Light of Togetherness

Our laughter mingles in the midnight air,
Tickling each other without a care.
You steal the covers; it's part of the game,
Calling me names with such playful fame.

In this moonlit scene, you take your stance,
Waging war while I sleep, not a chance.
The clock ticks slowly as we plot and scheme,
In our own little world, like a fever dream.

Your breath is a symphony, offbeat yet sweet,
I dance to the rhythm of your snoring repeat.
Unbroken moments drape the quiet room,
As we banter late into the night's bloom.

A chandelier of dreams sways above our plight,
As pillows become shields in our friendly fight.
The glow of your smile shines near and far,
As we chuckle in darkness, our own shining star.

Melodies Where the Darkness Sings

In the shadows, we compose our tune,
Dancing with echoes beneath the moon.
You're the maestro of this charming snore,
Conducting dreams, always wanting more.

Stars twinkle in rhythmic time to our play,
Cunningly sneaking snacks, night feels like day.
With each little giggle, the night bubbles bright,
We're pirates of slumber, floating in flight.

Your hair's like a nest where my thoughts entwine,
A crazy collection of dreams divine.
As your laugh shakes the walls with a playful boom,
I'll chart every whisper and sleep-ward loom.

In this cacophony of warmth and cheer,
The moon plays along; it's our stage right here.
Stealing kisses while the owl takes a stance,
In the melody's rhythm, we find our dance.

Nighthawks Coiled in Affection

We're two nighthawks with a wobbly flight,
Navigating dreams under dim starlight.
Your arm is a blanket, my fortress neat,
Yet somehow I still find your toes to defeat.

In this cozy nest, we trade sleepy grins,
As pillows become shields in our mischievous sins.
You tease me with dreams of breakfast in bed,
But first, let's resolve who snores instead.

We plot midnight feasts, with cookies galore,
Giggles erupt as we drop snacks on the floor.
In our quiet brawl, love's laughter sings,
With each clumsy moment, joy truly clings.

So here in our fortress, we build and collide,
With stars as our witness and laughter as guide.
In the twilight embrace, the world fades away,
As two nighthawks soar in their playful ballet.

Dreams Woven in the Dark

In shadows where we laugh and play,
The night conceals our silly ways.
With pillows stacked like mountain highs,
We dream of cupcakes in the skies.

A dance of giggles fills the room,
As starlit smiles disperse the gloom.
We twirl in blankets, fierce and bold,
Trading secrets that never get old.

The clock just laughs, it has no care,
For sleepy heads and wild hair.
In whispered tones, we plot to snack,
While scheming socks again go slack.

So here we lie, as dreams collide,
In this crazy world, you're my guide.
With you, the dark's a playful friend,
We'll weave these tales that never end.

Comfort Found in the Moon's Gaze

The moon peeks in, a cheeky guest,
With beams of light, it knows us best.
We share our snacks, our midnight feast,\nWhile making jokes, we laugh at least.

In cozy corners, we explore,
Where every shadow asks for more.
Your silly faces, masked in night,
Turn serious whispers into delight.

With cookies crumbled on the sheets,
We craft a world where laughter meets.
The moon winks down, it can't believe,
The goofy tales we dare conceive.

Through soft giggles, our worries fade,
In lunar glow, plans are laid.
Crafting dreams like kids at play,
We'll chase the stars until the day.

The Silence Between Heartbeats

In the hush where whispers dwell,
We create our own secret spell.
With a squeeze that says so much,
Laughter sparkles in every touch.

Just you and me, a playful tease,
Shushing sounds like rustling leaves.
We chase the giggles that won't stop,
As time holds still—let's flip the clock.

In clumsy moons we find our beat,
Our silly dances, a joyous feat.
The silence buzzes like a tease,
Where love and laughter find their ease.

So here we sit, no need for sound,
In this space, pure joy is found.
With every heartbeat, time we bend,
In the gaps, our giggles blend.

Embracing the Velvet Hour

As velvet drapes the world outside,
We slip away, no need to hide.
With laughter bubbling like warm stew,
In cozy corners, it's just us two.

The blanket fort, our fortress grand,
Filled with dreams concocted by hand.
With silly games and stories spun,
We steal away the night for fun.

The stars peer in with twinkling eyes,
Supporting all our playful lies.
In this embrace, we try to out-fun,
Tossing pillows till the day is won.

We may be lost, but we don't mind,
In this sweet chaos, laughter's blind.
With every chuckle, worry flees,
In the velvet hour, we find our ease.

Light's Embrace in Midnight's Hold

Beneath the moon, we giggle and tease,
Your breath tickles softly, a tickle of breeze.
Pajamas in patterns, oh what a sight,
Dancing shadows laugh, in the pale moonlight.

We swap silly stories, our feet on the floor,
Your popcorn skills need a little bit more.
Laughter erupts, like confetti in air,
Adventures unfold, like a well-thrown chair.

A culinary disaster, the cookies are burnt,
You made a sweet mess, oh how I've learned!
These nights fly by, like whispers on wings,
Each moment together, a treasure it brings.

In soft, playful chaos, we both find our place,
Tonight's an odd dance, a slow-motion race.
Wrapped in the joy, we forget the alarm,
In these hours we cherish, we're safe from all harm.

In the Sanctuary of Your Warmth

Wrapped in a blanket, we sprawl on the couch,
Your snoring's a symphony, sweet as a grouch.
With popcorn on faces, and crumbs down my shirt,
You wink, then you stumble, you land with a thud.

The clink of our mugs, caffeine rules the tunes,
We share our wild dreams with the stars and the moons.
You dance like a noodle, and I can't help but laugh,
While I try to pick up your silly giraffe.

Each tick of the clock is a game we play nice,
Life's rollercoaster caught in a slice.
The dark holds our secrets, they bubble like stew,
So here's to the mischief, just me and you.

With sock puppets ready, we put on a show,
A tale full of giggles that only we know.
In this cozy chaos, you're my favorite sound,
In the warmth of our world, endless laughter is found.

An Odyssey of Soft Starlight

In the glow of dim light, we plot our fun schemes,
You channel a pirate, I'm lost in daydreams.
Waves of our laughter, they crash on our cheeks,
As you fight with the couch for a snack, that's what we seek.

Your tales spin like silk, as the night keeps on rolling,
With ghosts in our shadows, their eerie controlling.
We jump at the creaks, but it's just silly nerves,
In this cozy cocoon, our love truly swerves.

A glass of some juice turns into a foam fight,
We're pirates, we're ninjas, we're lovers at night.
You challenge the stars, I'm your sidekick in crime,
In the rhythm of laughter, we dance out of time.

Through giggles and whispers, we conquer the dark,
Every tickle of fingers ignites a soft spark.
As the dawn starts to sneak in, we still won't depart,
With you by my side, oh, you've stolen my heart.

Interlaced Souls in the Quiet

The warmth of your laughter, my heartstrings do play,
As sunlight dips low, and the colors decay.
With popcorn explosions, and pillows like sails,
In ships made of dreams, we swap our bold tales.

Soft snorts and loud giggles, we roll on the floor,
You swipe all my snacks, then declare it a score!
In sleepy-eyed battles, with blankets as shields,
We fight for our dreams, in the softest of fields.

From fluff-ball discussions to whispers of fate,
It's you that I cherish, let's not hesitate.
With the clock ticking softly, our secrets will bloom,
Together in quiet, our hearts find their room.

As night closes gently, we nestle like kites,
You're the laugh of my days and the light of my nights.
So here's to our fortress, built high in the air,
In the sweet simple moments, together we share.

The Chill Alleviated by You

When winter winds do show their glee,
I find a spark, oh yes, in thee.
Your laughter warms the coldest air,
As snowflakes dance without a care.

We make hot chocolate, oh so sweet,
With marshmallows that dance and meet.
You spill it all, I laugh so loud,
Together we stand, a goofy crowd.

The blankets piled, a fort we build,
With popcorn scattered, hearts are thrilled.
As movie marathons start to play,
I'll steal the last chip, come what may!

So let the frostbite try its best,
With you, my dear, I'm truly blessed.
When giggles echo through the cold,
It's a warmth that can't be sold.

Echoing Whispers in the Stillness

In the quiet hush, you whisper jokes,
Your punchlines hit like playful pokes.
The stars above roll their bright eyes,
As we burst out with silly sighs.

Your snoring's like a freight train's song,
But in this chaos, I belong.
You snuggle close, I give a nudge,
And in the dark, we both begrudge.

Illuminated by moonlit beams,
We hatch our wildest midnight schemes.
We dream of pies and dance on dreams,
While sipping soda, bursting seams.

So let the stillness wrap us tight,
With goofy giggles, pure delight.
In shadowed corners, we just smile,
Creating joy that lasts a while.

Embracing the Veil of Night

The moon's a clown, it shines so bright,
While we juggle shadows of the night.
Your silly face, a comical sight,
Makes every heartbeat feel just right.

We dance like fools without a care,
In pajamas that we both can share.
As laughter bubbles and softly grows,
We slip and slide on toes and woes.

We whisper secrets, giggle and tease,
As the night sways like gentle breeze.
With each goofy story that we tell,
I realize, this is my special spell.

So here we are, wrapped up in fun,
Two silly souls, we've truly won.
As stars waltz by, we sway and sway,
Embracing the love in our own way.

Beyond the Horizon of Shadows

In the shadows where giggles play,
We chase the gloom, we shoo it away.
Your chortle's like a thunder clap,
It fills the night, a cheerful map.

With flashlights flashing, ducks in tow,
We dance like pros, though feet are slow.
The world outside might seem so dark,
But with your light, we'll hit the park.

So let's embark on our silly ride,
With whoopee cushions as our pride.
The horizon laughs and dances too,
With every quirk, it celebrates you.

Beyond the shadows, laughter calls,
We build our castles, even if they fall.
In the realm of fun, where night does gleam,
Together, my love, we weave a dream.